MULTIPLICATION FUN PRACTICE BOOK

PART 2

FAIR USE OF THIS PRODUCT

At MegaGeex, we love making content designed to help build better learners. Our resources empower parents and educators alike to give kids hands-on inspiration to grow into the world-changing adults we want them to be. To be able to do that, we need your help to guarantee that we have the resources to continue to create great content.

If our resources are used beyond home and personal use, in a classroom, or other educational settings where you receive compensation, then a professional license is required.

Each professional license allows for a single teacher to use the resource for students in the teacher's class or block of classes. Price is determined by the number of students using the resource. If more than one teacher in your school wants access to the materials, then additional licenses are available for purchase.

Questions? Feel free to reach out to us at hello@megageex.com and we'll be happy to help. If someone you know would like to use one of our printable pages, have them check out www.megageex.com for our full catalog.

As always, we thank you for your support, and for granting us the ability to help you build a better future through today's little learners.

Hello!

If we could look back over 600 years, most would be amazed at the developments, discoveries, and inventions that have changed the world. Human-kind, in this small space of time, has made advancements in every area of our lives. Communication is possible with people thousands of miles away- in real time! Circling the planet is accomplished in only days. Television, movies, computers, automobiles, only begin to tell the story of the mind-blowing improvements that benefit us all.

These awesome accomplishments were made possible by regular people who had extraordinary qualities. Men and women who shared two common traits: Passion and Grit. In the face of challenges and even failures, they never quit, and they succeeded in what many viewed as impossible.

With dedication and persistence, they overcame whatever hurdles given to them by society during their lives. Women such as Ada Lovelace, Marie Curie, and Jane Austen pursued their education despite laws and views that said they could not. George Washington Carver never gave up in the face of racial discrimination. And Albert Einstein could not find a job as a professor but he still continued work on his theories. These are just a few examples of the character of these remarkable individuals.

In 2018, Daniel Scalosub, embarked on a mission of his own. He wanted his twin daughters to know that they can do ANYTHING. And what better way to prove this to them than to share the incredible stories of these inventors, writers, scientists and artists, and entrepreneurs. Daniel founded Megageex to bring knowledge, and more importantly, inspiration and encouragement to kids everywhere.

Feel free to explore our unique products. Each one is designed with the sole purpose to inspire and teach through play and creativity.

Connect your kids with the world's greatest minds and get ready for a learning journey like no other.

Welcome to Megageex!

Nikola Tesla

Serbian scientist, inventor, and futurist (1856 - 1942). Designed the alternating current (AC) model that provides electricity to homes. Pioneered radio transmissions and wireless technology.

Rosalind Franklin

English chemist (1920 - 1958). Proved the double-helix model of DNA, the building blocks of all life. Her work on the structure of viruses contributed to founding the field of structural virology.

Thomas Edison

American inventor and entrepreneur (1847 - 1931). Considered "America's greatest inventor". Invented the light bulb, the phonograph, the first motion picture camera, early electric power generators, and over a thousand other inventions.

George Washington Carver

American agricultural chemist and agronomist (1860s - 1942). Developed methods for improving soil fertility, and crops versatility. Created products with peanuts, which gave him the nickname "the Peanut Man".

Galileo Galilei

Italian scientist (1564 - 1642). Considered the "father of modern physics". Pioneered the "scientific method" of learning through observation, asking questions and seeking answers by doing experiments.

The Wright Brothers

American aviation pioneers and inventors (Orville 1871 - 1948, Wilbur 1867 - 1912). They invented and built the first motorized airplane and were the first men to fly it in December 1903.

Isaac Newton

English mathematician and scientist (1642 - 1727). Formulated the laws of gravity, motion, and energy. Developed calculus, a new type of math for understanding and describing continuous change.

Madam CJ Walker

American businesswoman, entrepreneur, and social activist (1867 - 1919). Created the first cosmetics and hair care line of products for African-American women. First self-made American female millionaire.

Wolfgang Amadeus Mozart

Austrian composer and child prodigy (1756 - 1791). Considered one of the most popular composers in western history, having composed more than 600 works. His music had a tremendous influence on subsequent western music.

Alexander Graham Bell

Scottish scientist, inventor, and teacher of the deaf (1847 - 1922). Invented the first practical telephone and founded AT&T, the world's first telephone company.

Jane Austen

English writer and author (1775 - 1817) who wrote such classic books as Pride & Prejudice, Emma, and Sense & Sensibility which challenged country life in 1800s century England.

Charles Darwin

English naturalist and biologist (1809 - 1882). Pioneered the science of evolution. His work *On the Origin of Species* shows how beings evolve over time through natural selection.

Ada Lovelace

English mathematician and writer (1815 - 1852). Regarded as the "world's first computer programmer". Wrote the first computer algorithm based on Charles Babbage's Analytical Machine.

Leonardo Da Vinci

Italian inventor, artist, and naturalist (1452 - 1519) whose wide-ranging works include the Mona Lisa, the first helicopter, and is considered one of the most brilliant people to have ever lived.

Alan Turing

English mathematician (1912 - 1954). Considered the "father of computer science" and pioneered artificial intelligence. Built early computers to break German codes and help win World War II.

Marie Curie

Polish physicist and chemist (1867 - 1934). The first woman to win the Nobel Prize for her discovery of radioactivity, and the first person to win the Nobel twice. Discovered the elements radium and polonium.

Albert Einstein

German physicist (1879 - 1955). One of the world's most influential scientists, whose work on light, gravity, time and space changed the way we understand our universe. Formulated the Theory of Relativity and Nobel Prize winner in Physics.

MULTIPLICATION TABLE

Albert Einstein →

← Marie Curie

X	1	2	3	4	5	6	7	8	9	10	11	12
1	1	2	3	4	5	6	7	8	9	10	11	12
2	2	4	6	8	10	12	14	16	18	20	22	24
3	3	6	9	12	15	18	21	24	27	30	33	36
4	4	8	12	16	20	24	28	32	36	40	44	48
5	5	10	15	20	25	30	35	40	45	50	55	60
6	6	12	18	24	30	36	42	48	54	60	66	72
7	7	14	21	28	35	42	49	56	63	70	77	84
8	8	16	24	32	40	48	56	64	72	80	88	96
9	9	18	27	36	45	54	63	72	81	90	99	108
10	10	20	30	40	50	60	70	80	90	100	110	120
11	11	22	33	44	55	66	77	88	99	110	121	132
12	12	24	36	48	60	72	84	96	108	120	132	144

   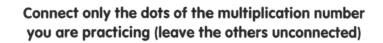

Connect only the dots of the multiplication number you are practicing (leave the others unconnected)

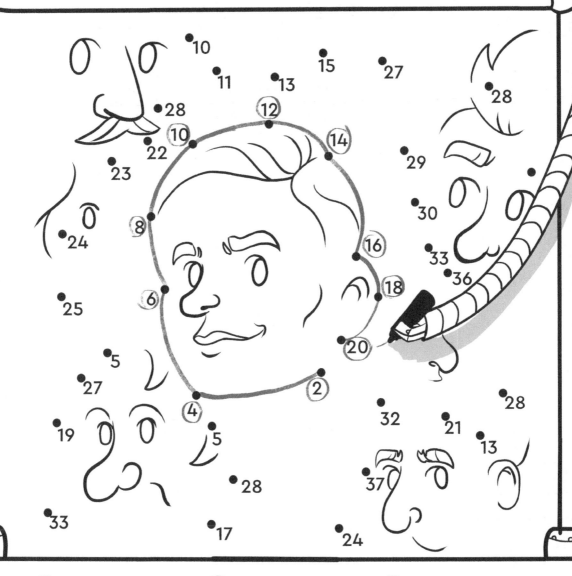

2x1 = ②	2x4 = ⑧	2x7 = ⑭	
2x2 = ④	2x5 = ⑩	2x8 = ⑯	2x10 = ⑳
2x3 = ⑥	2x6 = ⑫	2x9 = ⑱	

11

" It's OK not to know. It's not ok not to try. "

Ada Lovelace

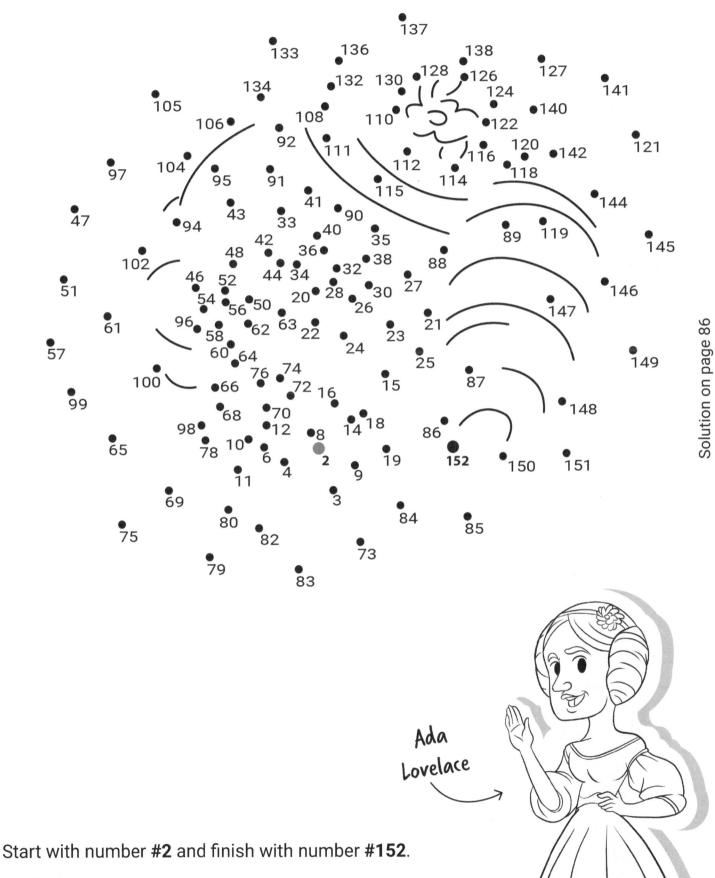

Solution on page 86

Start with number **#2** and finish with number **#152**.

13

"Every mistake you make is progress. "

George Washington Carver

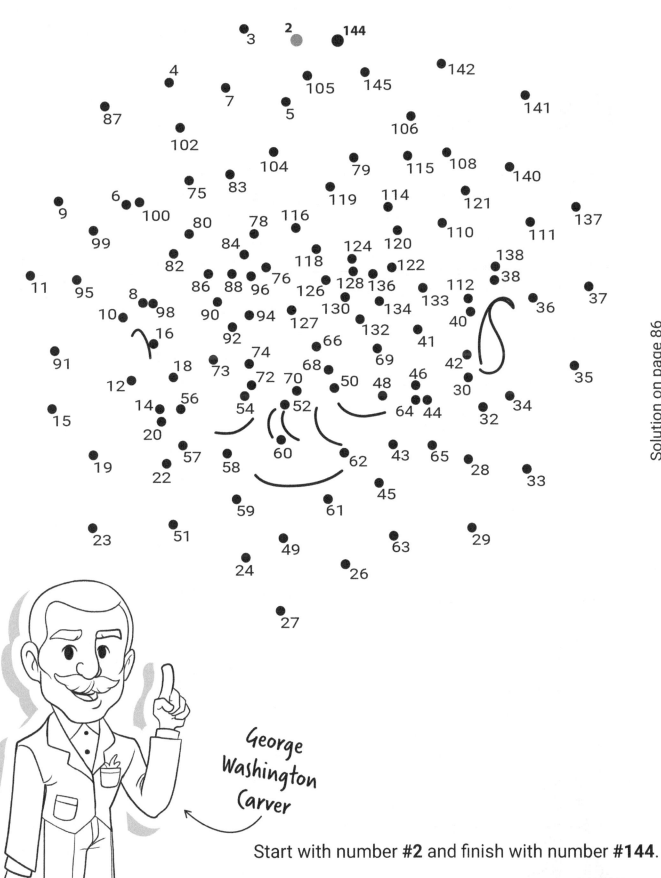

Solution on page 86

Start with number **#2** and finish with number **#144**.

George
Washington
Carver

"The best way to *predict* the future is to *create* it.

ABRAHAM LINCOLN "

Nikola
Tesla

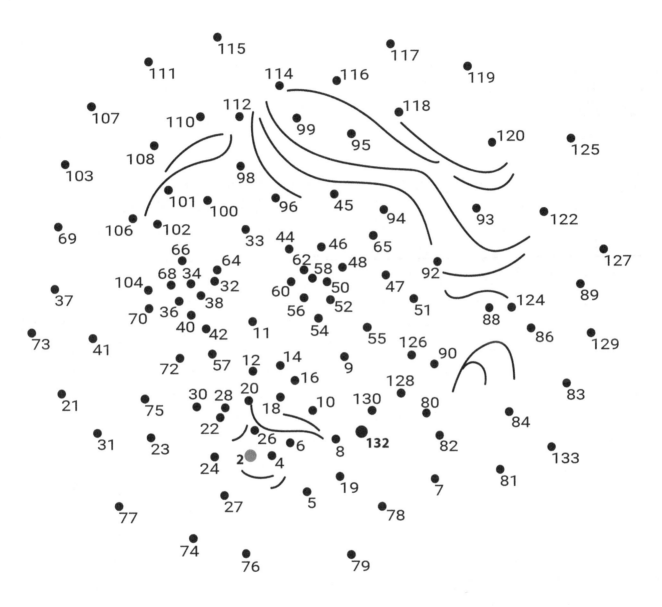

Solution on page 86

Nikola Tesla

Start with number **#2** and finish with number **#132**.

I've **learned** that I have a lot to **learn.**

MAYA ANGELOU

Thomas Edison

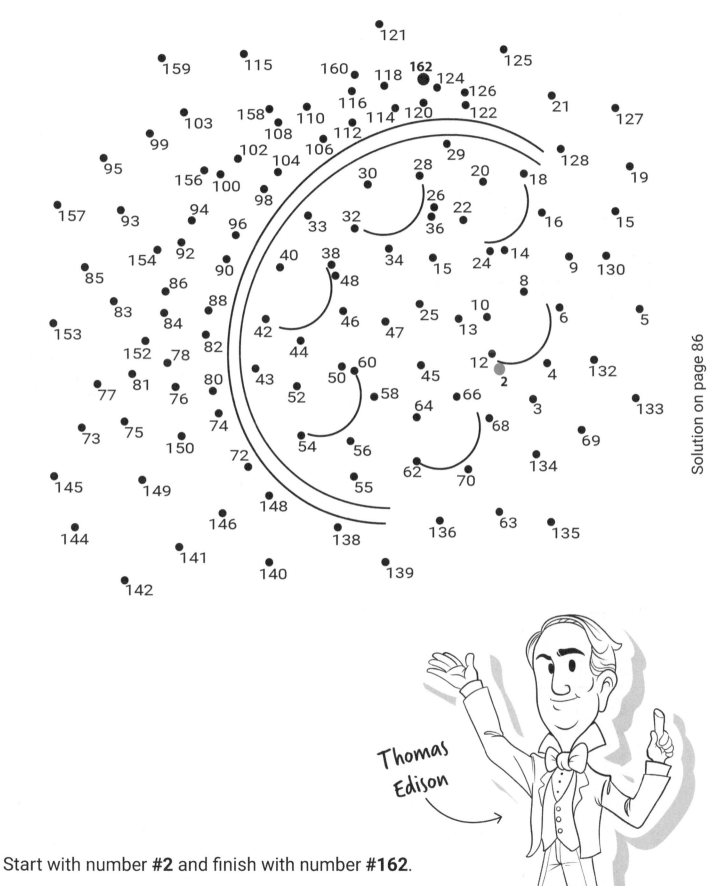

Solution on page 86

Start with number **#2** and finish with number **#162**.

19

" I got my *start* by giving *myself* a start.

MADAM CJ WALKER "

Madam C.J. Walker

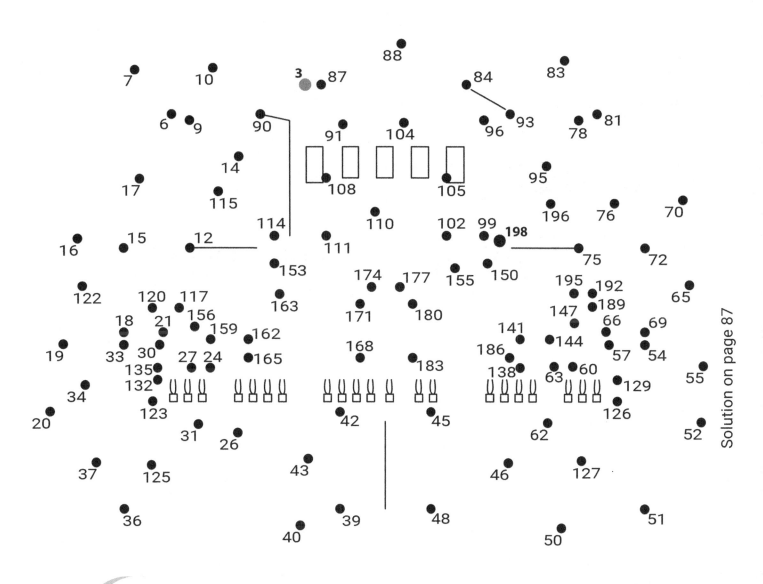

Solution on page 87

Madam
C.J. Walker

Start with number **#3** and finish with number **#198**.

"Change your THOUGHTS and CHANGE the world.

Alan Turing

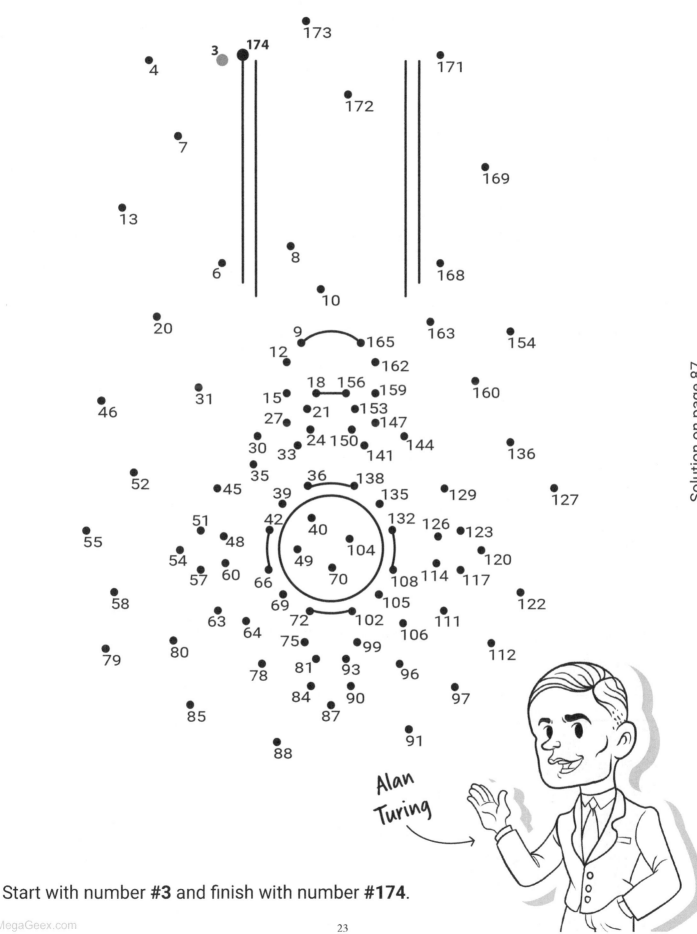

Solution on page 87

Start with number **#3** and finish with number **#174**.

" If you can dream it, you can do it. "

Leonardo Da Vinci

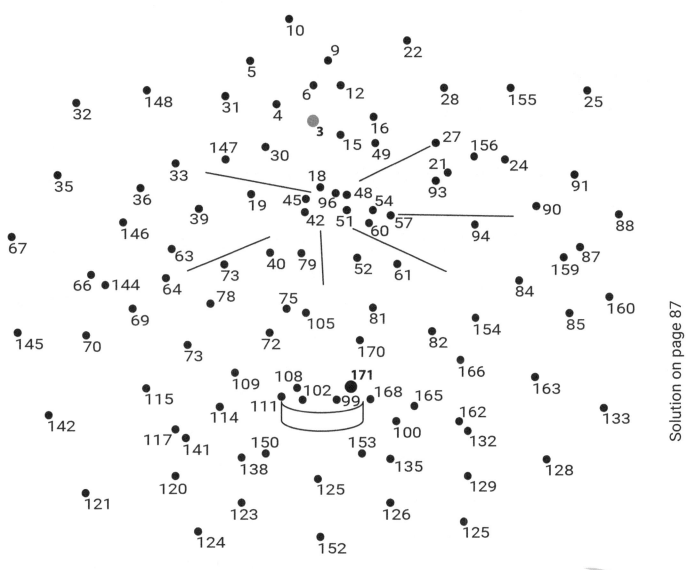

Solution on page 87

Leonardo
Da Vinci

Start with number **#3** and finish with number **#171**.

25

" In the middle of DIFFICULTY lies OPPORTUNITY!

ALBERT EINSTEIN "

Albert
Einstein

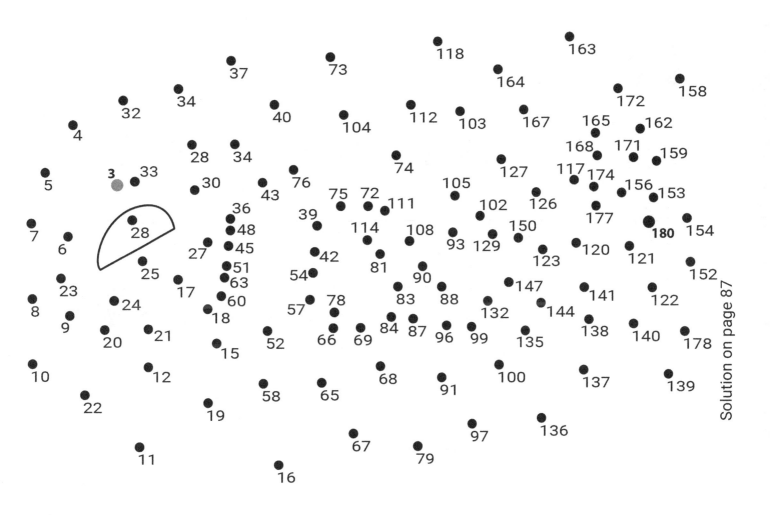

Solution on page 87

Albert
Einstein

Start with number **#3** and finish with number **#180**.

> **"** **Failure** is not the **opposite** of success. It's a **part** of it.
>
> ARIANNA HUFFINGTON **"**

Wolfgang Amadeus Mozart

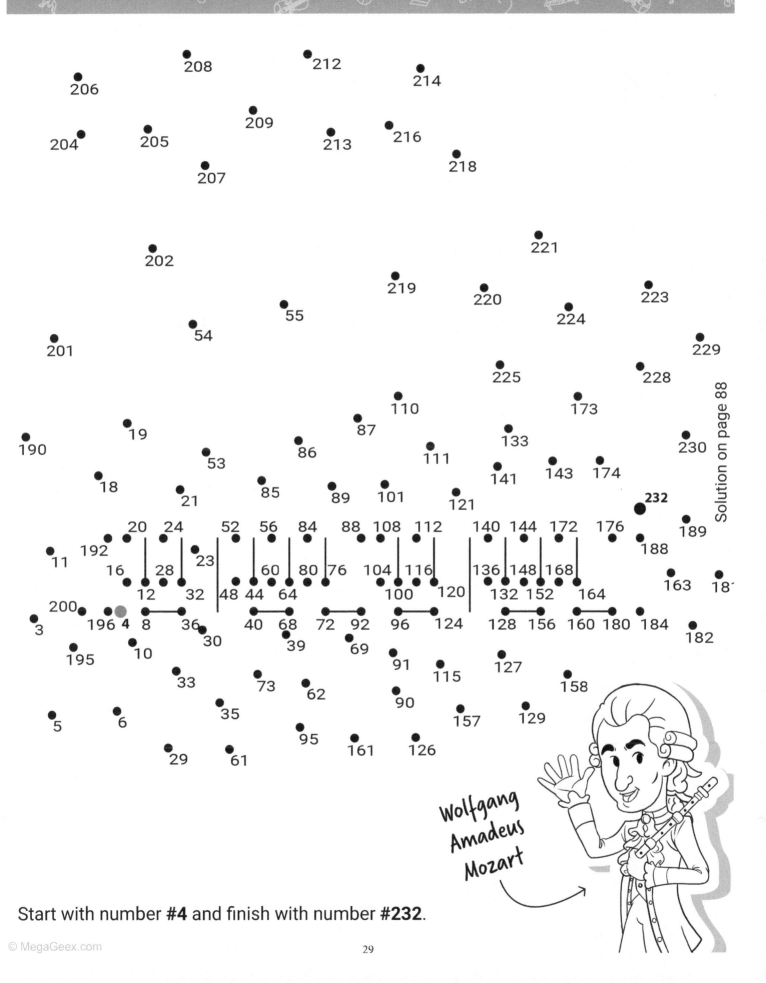

Solution on page 88

Start with number **#4** and finish with number **#232**.

> "Take the first step in faith. You don't have to see the whole staircase, just take the first step.
>
> **MARTIN LUTHER KING** "

Isaac Newton

Solution on page 88

Isaac Newton

Start with number **#4** and finish with number **#196**.

© MegaGeex.com

" It does not matter how slowly you go so long as you do *NOT STOP*. "

CONFUCIUS

The Wright Brothers

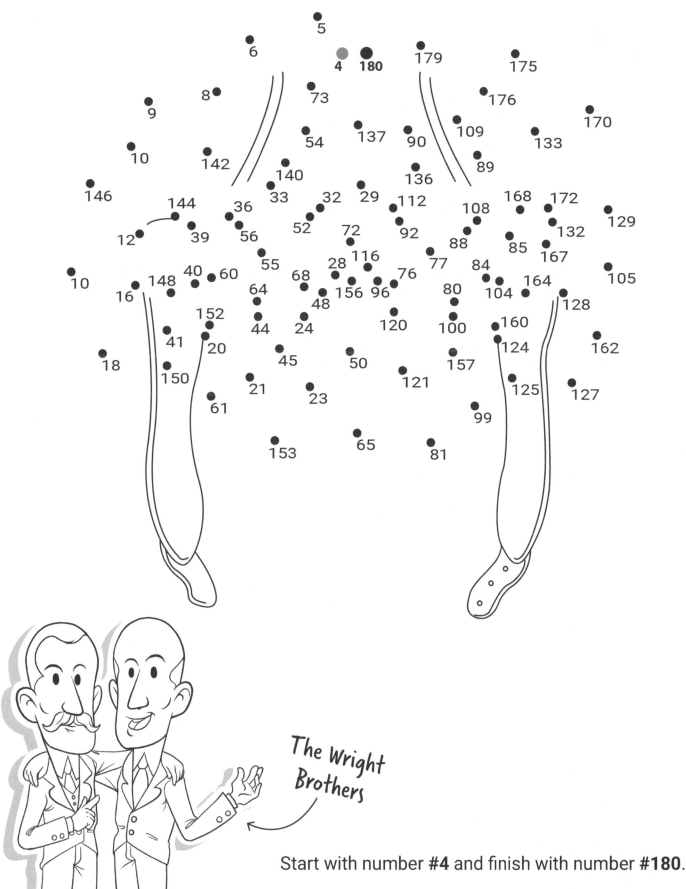

Solution on page 88

The Wright Brothers

Start with number **#4** and finish with number **#180**.

© MegaGeex.com

"Challenges are what make life INTERESTING. Overcoming them is what makes life MEANINGFUL.

JOSHUA J. MARINE "

Marie Curie

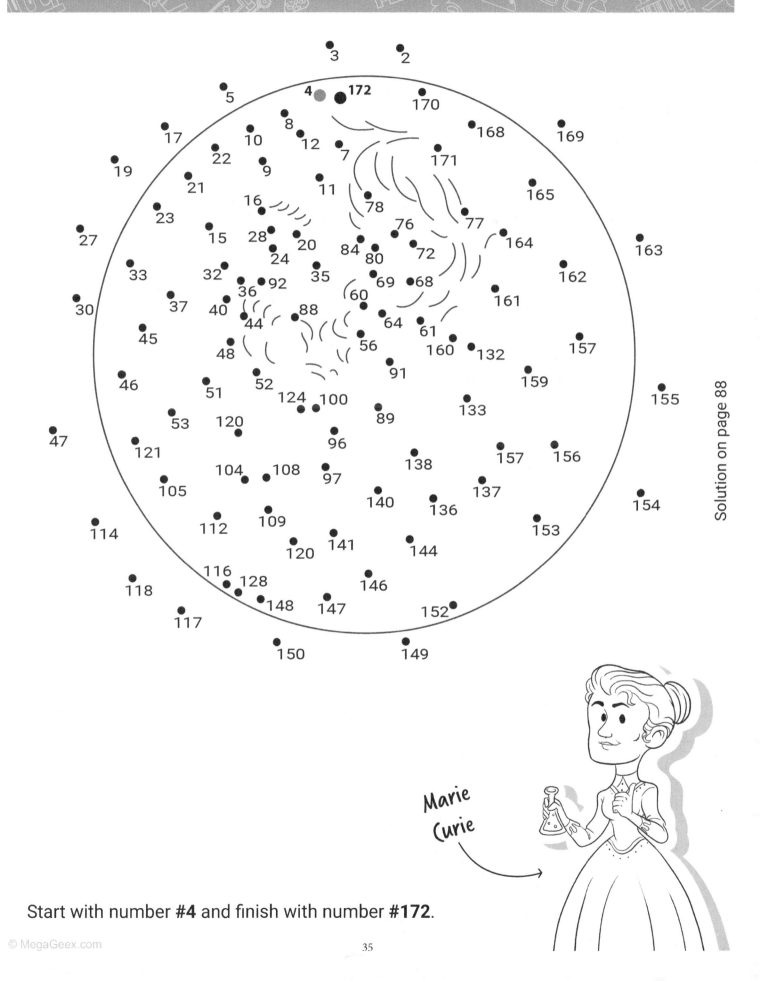

Solution on page 88

Start with number **#4** and finish with number **#172**.

"Somewhere, something incredible is waiting to be known."

CARL SAGAN "

Charles Darwin

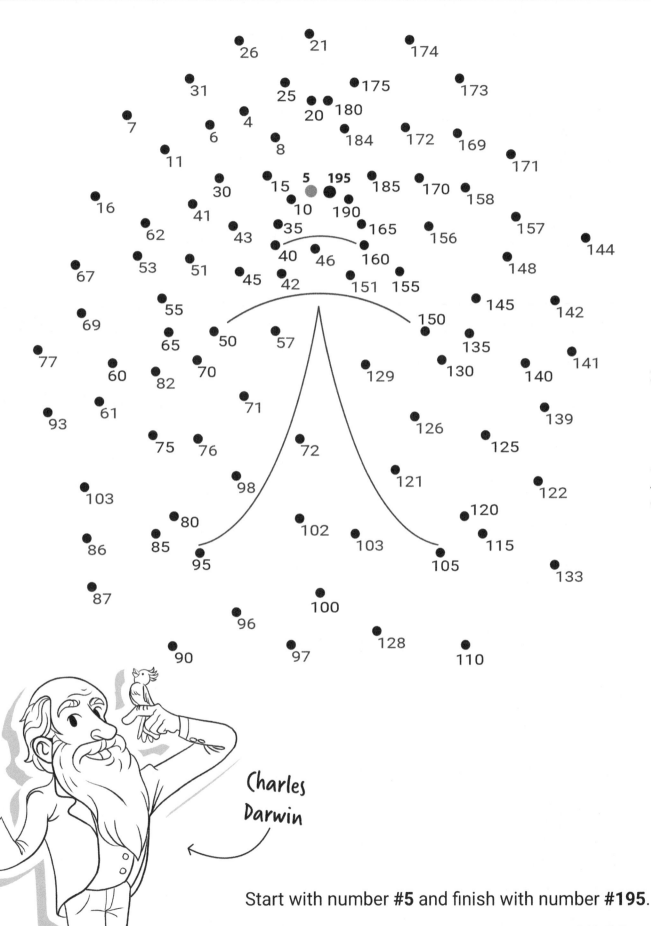

Solution on page 89

Charles Darwin

Start with number **#5** and finish with number **#195**.

© MegaGeex.com

"Always *DO* what you are *afraid* of doing. "

RALPH WALDO EMERSON

The Wright Brothers

Solution on page 89

The Wright Brothers

Start with number **#5** and finish with number **#185**.

"If it doesn't challenge you, it won't change you.

FRED DEVITO **"**

Ada
Lovelace

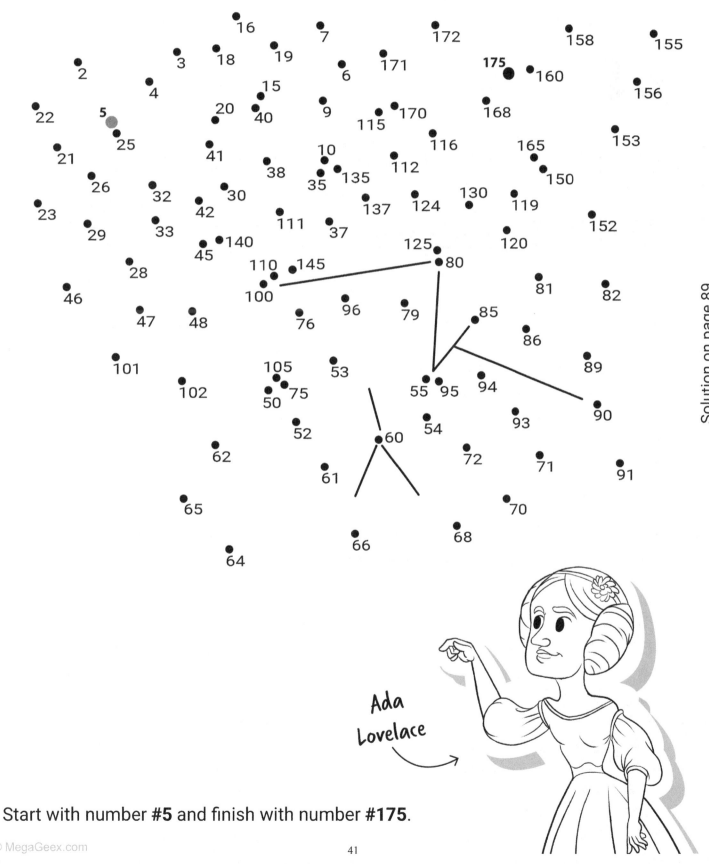

Solution on page 89

Ada
Lovelace

Start with number **#5** and finish with number **#175**.

Every **problem** is a gift.

Without them we wouldn't **GROW**.

Alexander
Graham Bell

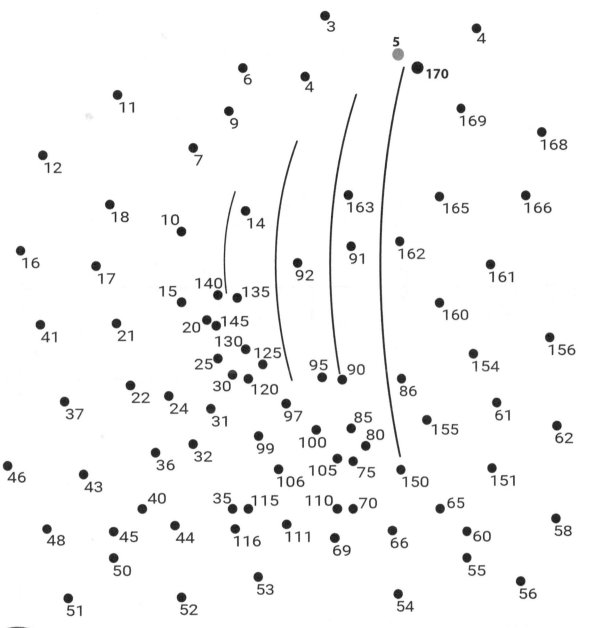

Solution on page 89

Alexander
Graham Bell

Start with number **#5** and finish with number **#170**.

43

"Failure is success if we learn from it.

MALCOLM FORBES "

Rosalind Franklin

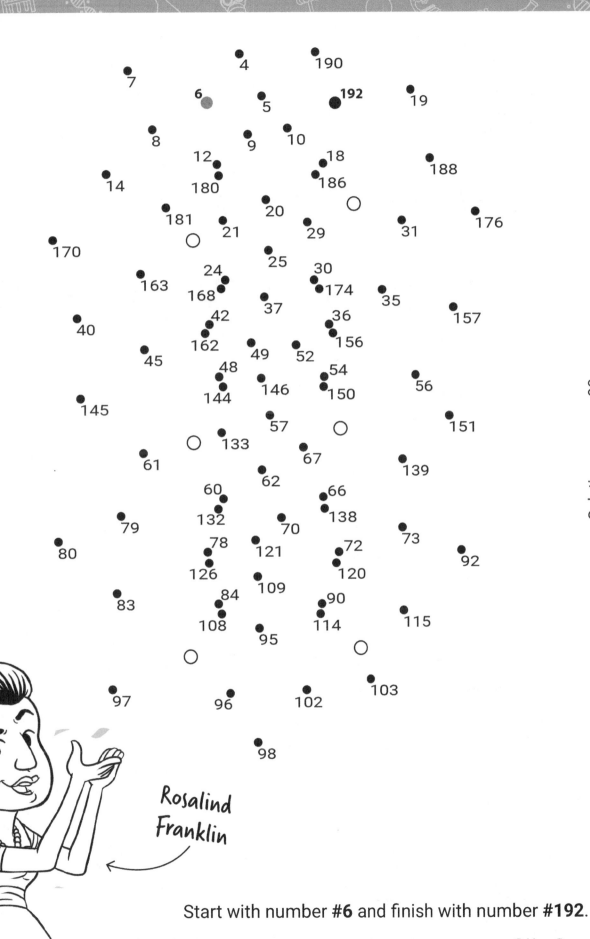

Rosalind
Franklin

Solution on page 90

Start with number #6 and finish with number #192.

© MegaGeex.com

No one is PERFECT. That's why pencils have ERASERS.

WOLFGANG RIEBE

Jane Austen

Solution on page 90

Start with number **#6** and finish with number **#192**.

"Education is the key to unlocking the golden door to freedom.

GEORGE WASHINGTON CARVER

George Washington Carver

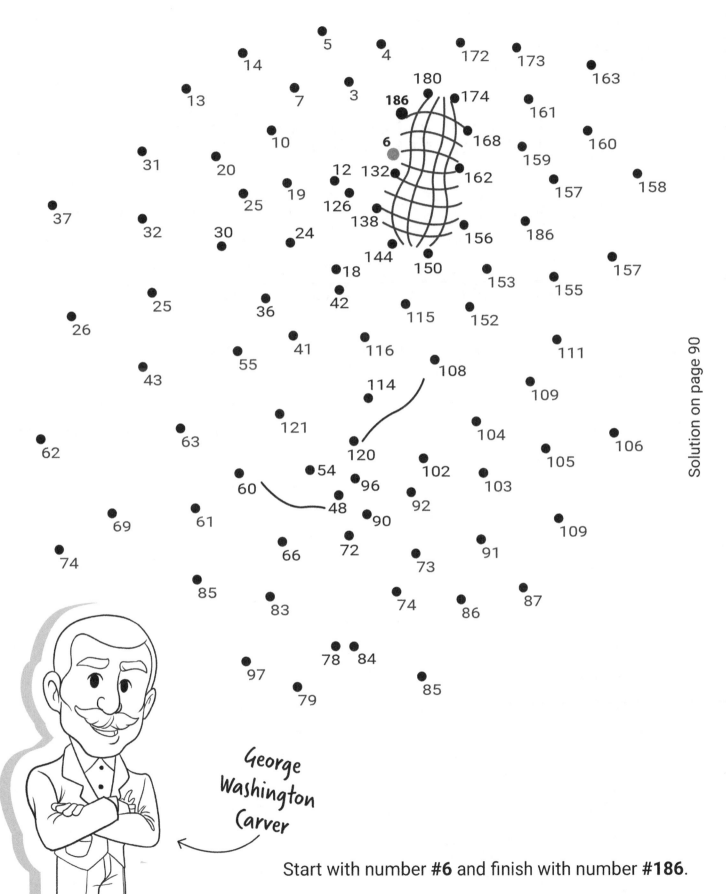

Solution on page 90

George
Washington
Carver

Start with number **#6** and finish with number **#186**.

© MegaGeex.com

" I am always doing what I *cannot* do yet. In order to *learn* how to do it.

VINCENT VAN GOGH "

Wolfgang Amadeus Mozart

Solution on page 90

Start with number #7 and finish with number #203.

Wolfgang Amadeus Mozart

> " All **TRUTHS** are easy to understand once they are discovered, the point is to **DISCOVER** them.
>
> GALILEO "

Galileo Galilei

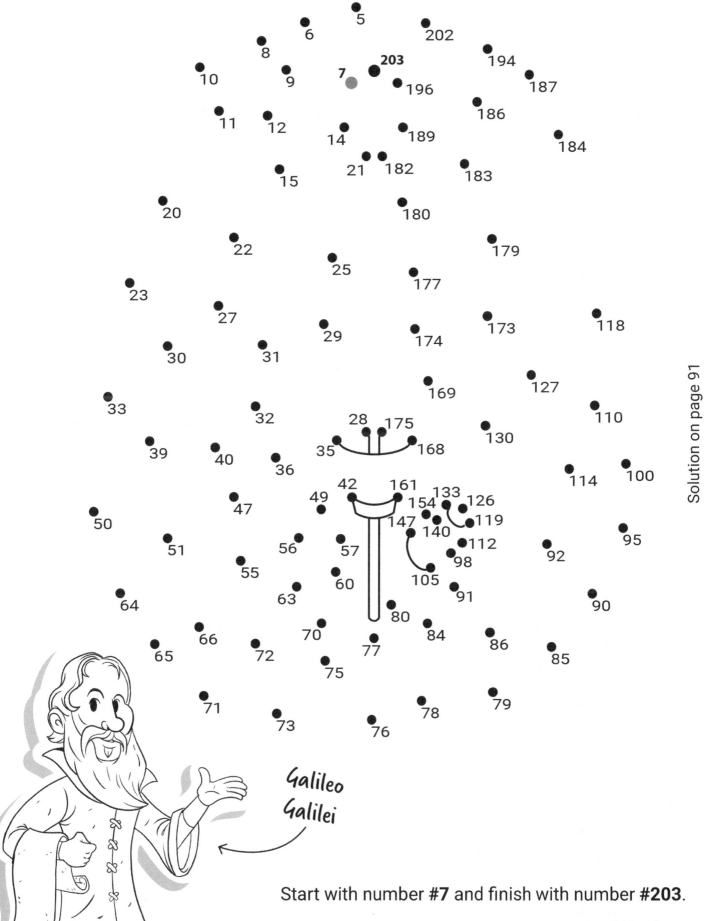

Solution on page 91

Galileo Galilei

Start with number #7 and finish with number #203.

"Learning is a treasure that will follow its owner everywhere.

CHINESE PROVERB 99

Isaac Newton

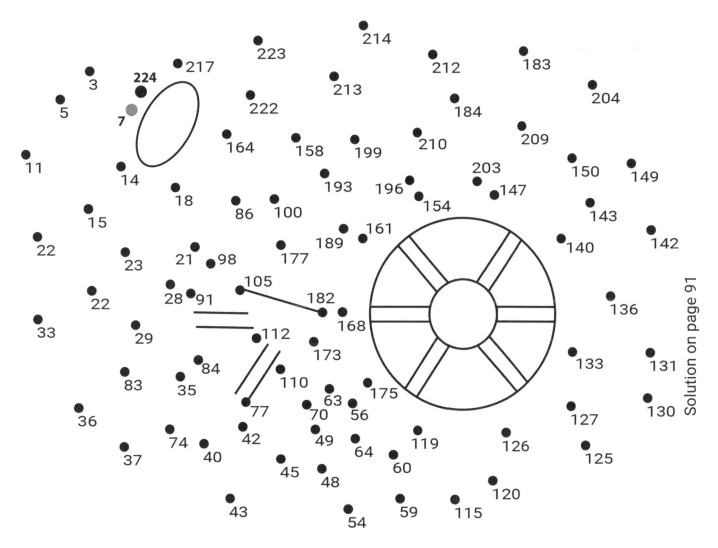

Isaac
Newton

Start with number **#7** and finish with number **#224**.

"

It's not that I'm so **SMART**,
it's just that I stay
with problems **LONGER**.

ALBERT EINSTEIN "

Albert
Einstein

Solution on page 91

Start with number #8 and finish with number #240.

> " I am not afraid of storms, for I am learning to sail my ship.

LITTLE WOMEN "

Ada Lovelace

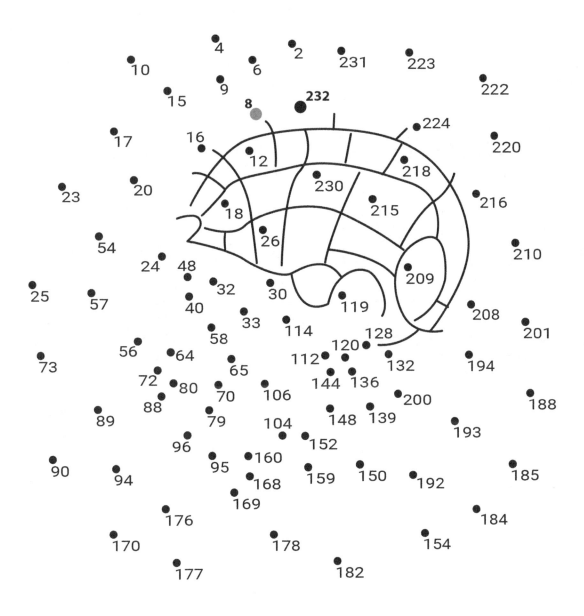

Solution on page 91

Ada
Lovelace

Start with number #8 and finish with number #232.

59

> "If you find a path with no **obstacles**, it probably doesn't lead **anywhere**.

FRANK A. CLARK "

Alan Turing

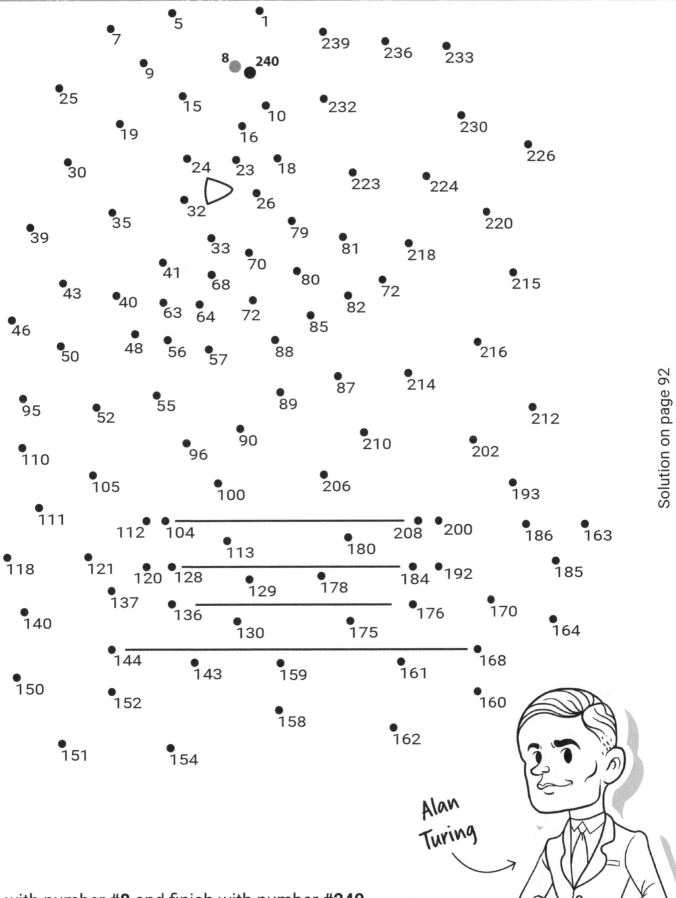

Solution on page 92

Start with number **#8** and finish with number **#240**.

"

Always turn a 𝕟𝕖𝕘𝕒𝕥𝕚𝕧𝕖 situation into a 𝕡𝕠𝕤𝕚𝕥𝕚𝕧𝕖 situation.

MICHAEL JORDAN "

Marie
Curie

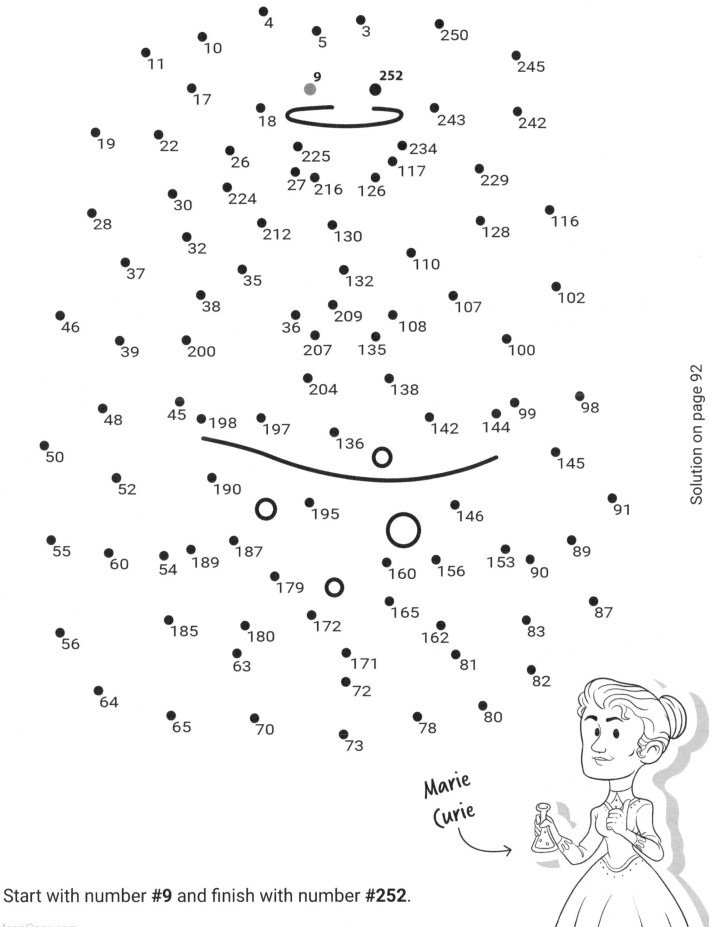

Solution on page 92

Marie Curie

Start with number #9 and finish with number #252.

"I am 87 and I am still LEARNING.

MICHELANGELO "

Thomas Edison

Solution on page 92

Start with number **#9** and finish with number **#234**.

" Whatever you are, be a good one.

ABRAHAM LINCOLN "

Charles Darwin

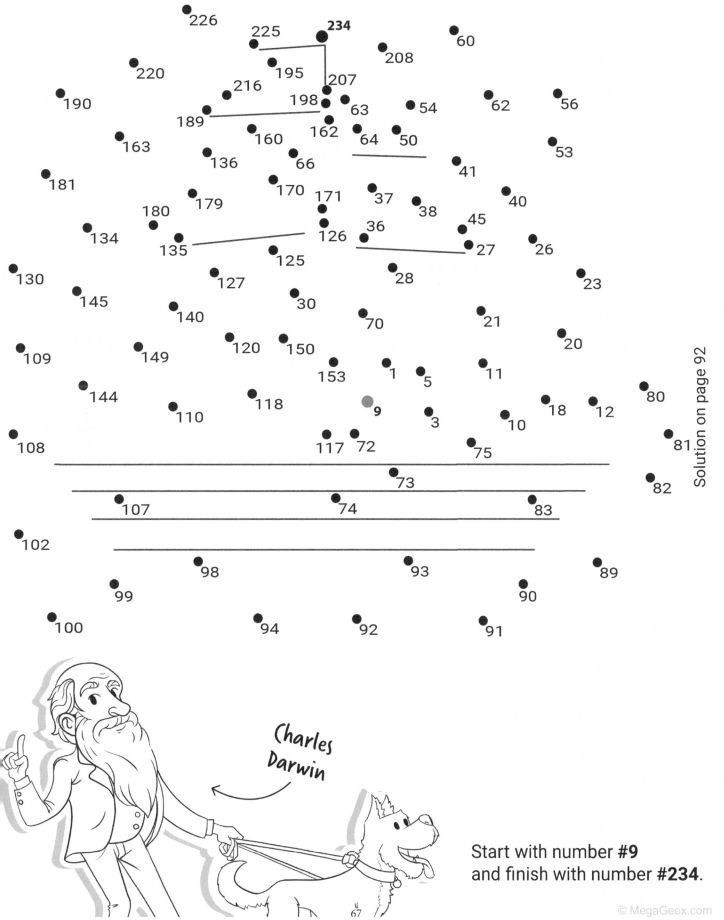

Charles Darwin

Start with number **#9**
and finish with number **#234**.

Solution on page 92

© MegaGeex.com

Do not judge me by
my successes, judge me by
how many times I fell
and got back up again.

NELSON MANDELA

Nikola
Tesla

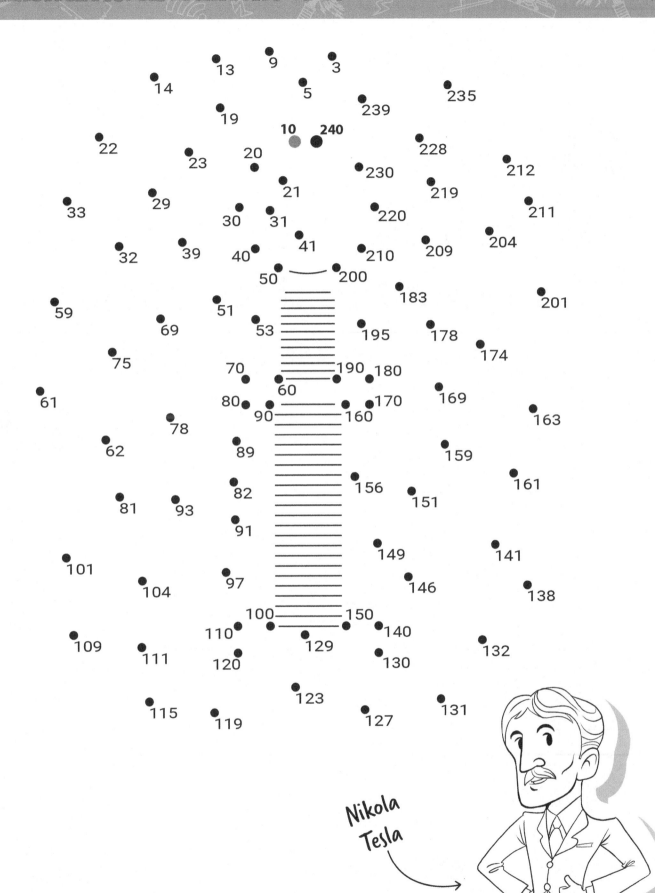

Solution on page 93

Nikola Tesla

Start with number #10 and finish with number #240.

"We can do ANYTHING we want to if we stick to it LONG enough.

HELEN KELLER **"**

Madam C.J. Walker

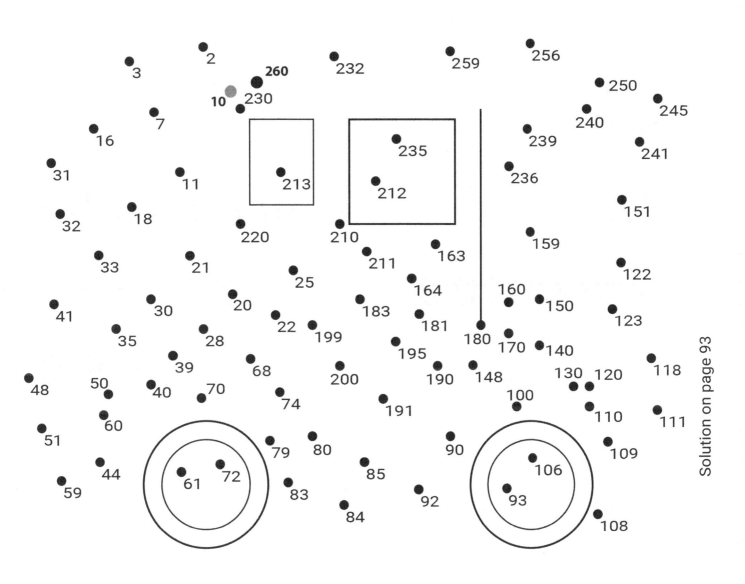

3
2
260
10 230
7
16
31
11
18
32
33
21
41
30
20
35
28
39
68
50
40
70
48
60
51
44
59
61 72
79 80
74
83
84
85
220
25
22
199
200
191
213
210
211
183
195
190
92
235
212
163
164
181
180 170 140
148 130 120
100
90
106
93
108
110
109
118
111
123
150
160
159
236
239
240
151
122
256
259
232
250
245
241

Madam
C.J. Walker

Start with number **#10** and finish with number **#260**.

"The **expert** in anything was once a **beginner.**

HELEN HAYES "

Galileo Galilei

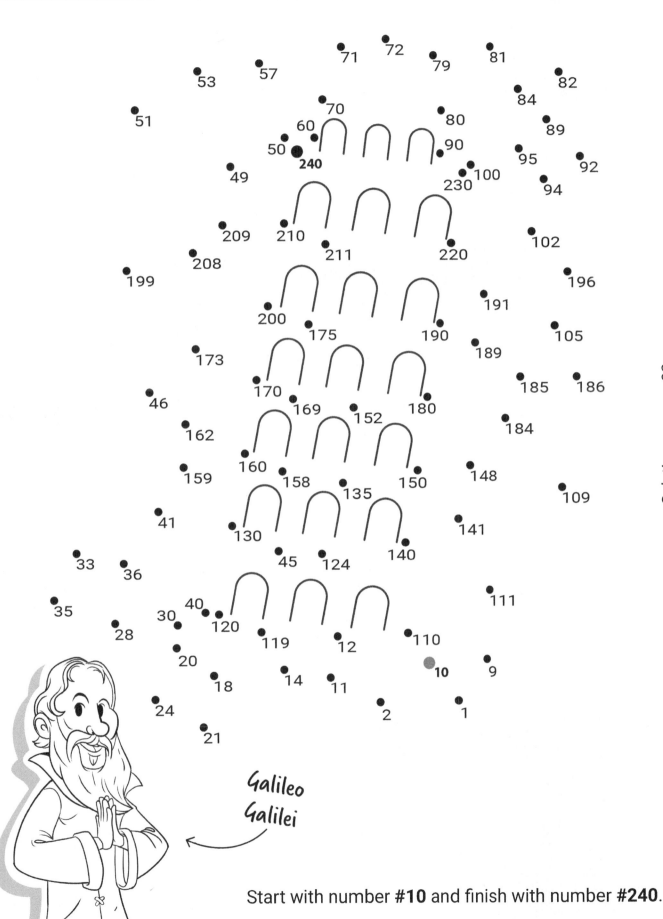

Galileo
Galilei

Solution on page 93

Start with number **#10** and finish with number **#240**.

© MegaGeex.com

" I think it's *possible* for ordinary people to choose to be *extraordinary*.

ELON MUSK **"**

Alexander
Graham Bell

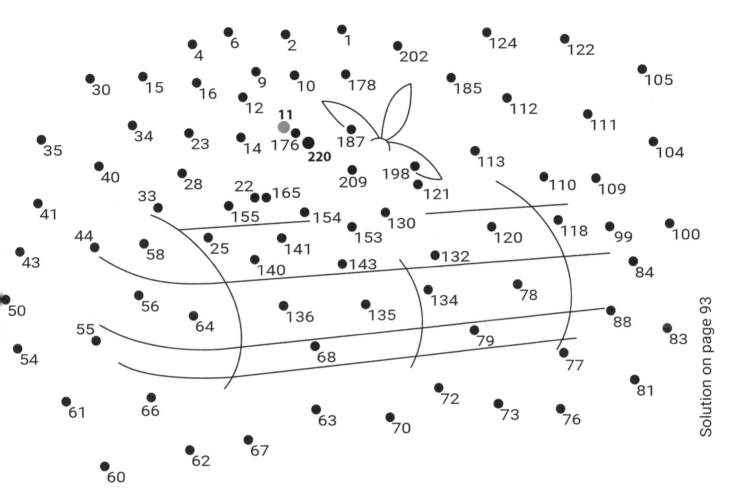

Solution on page 93

Alexander
Graham Bell

Start with number **#11** and finish with number **#220**.

© MegaGeex.com

"
The secret to getting *ahead* is getting *started*.

MARK TWAIN **"**

Rosalind Franklin

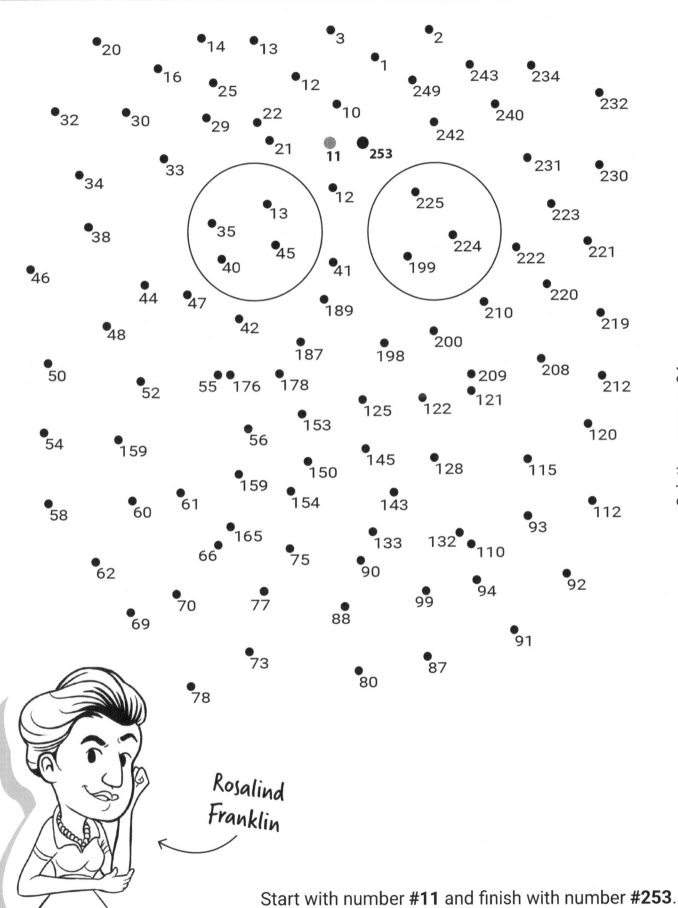

Solution on page 94

Rosalind
Franklin

Start with number **#11** and finish with number **#253**.

"
If at first you don't succeed... you're NORMAL!

KID PRESIDENT
"

Albert Einstein

Solution on page 94

Start with number #11 and finish with number #176.

Albert Einstein

"

Go **CONFIDENTLY** in the direction
of your **DREAMS.**
Live the life you have **IMAGINED.**

HENRY DAVID THOREAU **"**

Jane
Austen

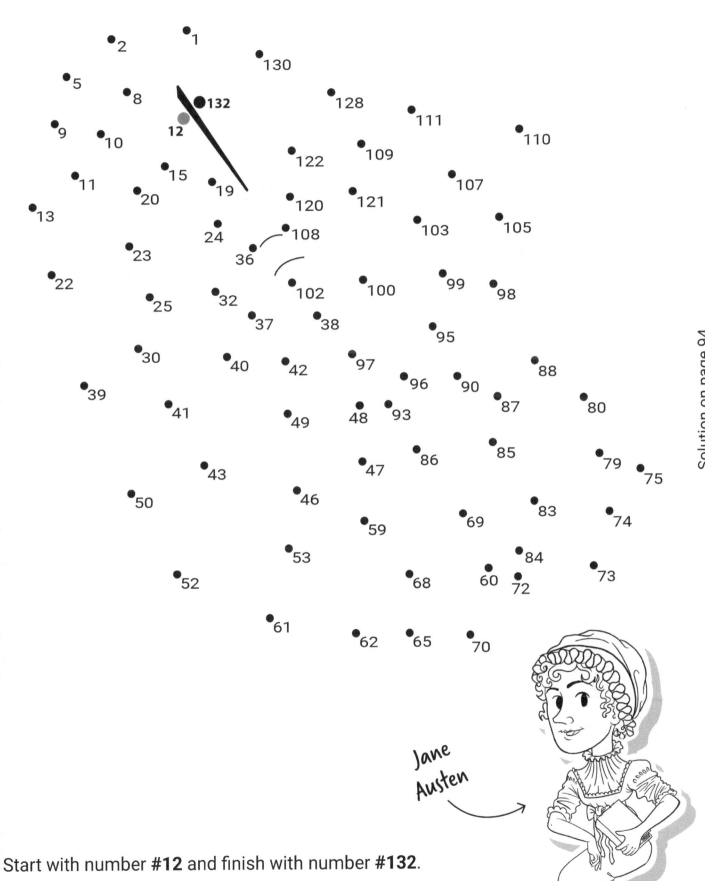

Solution on page 94

Start with number #12 and finish with number #132.

"**I GROW** my brain by **LEARNING** hard things."

Charles
Darwin

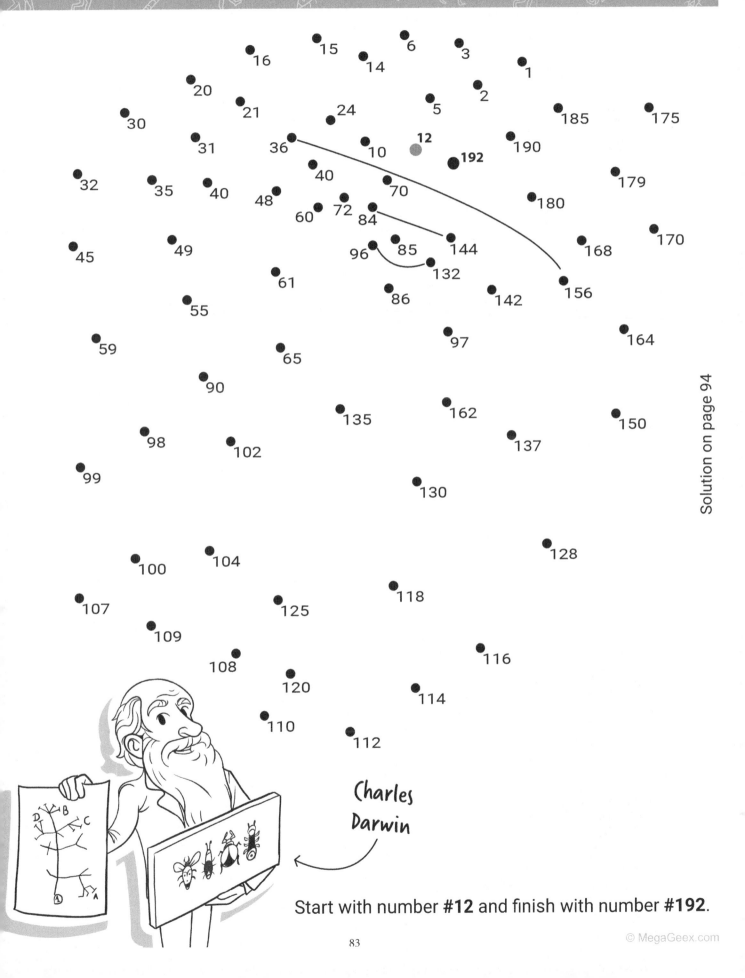

15

16

6

3

14

1

20

2

21

24

5

30

185

175

31

36

10

12

190

32

40

192

179

35

40

70

180

48

45

49

72

84

144

168

170

60

96

85

132

61

86

142

156

55

97

164

59

65

90

162

135

150

98

137

102

99

130

128

100

104

118

107

125

116

109

108

120

114

110

112

Charles
Darwin

Solution on page 94

Start with number **#12** and finish with number **#192**.

83

© MegaGeex.com

" Be the CHANGE you want to see in the WORLD.

GANDHI **"**

Leonardo
Da Vinci

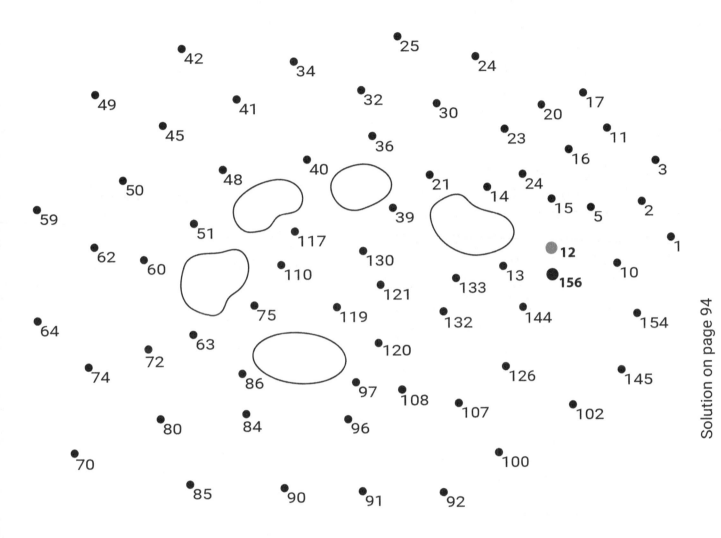

42

34

25

24

49

41

32

30

17

45

20

11

36

23

16

3

40

48

21

14

24

50

51

39

15

5

2

59

117

130

12

1

62

110

133

13

156

10

60

121

75

119

132

144

154

64

63

72

120

126

145

74

86

97

107

102

84

108

100

80

96

70

85

90

91

92

Solution on page 94

Leonardo
Da Vinci

Start with number **#12** and finish with number **#156**.

Page 13

Ada Lovelace

Ada Lovelace, born in 1815, is considered the First Computer Programmer. Many women did not have a formal education in her time, but Lovelace excelled in mathematics. She developed algorithms that convert letters to numerical data. She created computer code before computers were invented!

Page 15

George Washington Carver

As a Black man, George Washington Carver was not allowed to attend universities. He never gave up, and he became an agricultural scientist. He developed ways to improve soil that was no longer rich and healthy due to so many years of growing cotton.

Page 17

Nikola Tesla

Nikola Tesla had a passion for electricity. He invented the first alternating current (AC) motor and the technology that generates and transmits alternating currents. With this invention, electric power that is generated can travel long distances.

Page 19

Film roll

Edison's laboratory produced the first motion picture film camera called the Kinetograph. The first film Edison produced, called *Monkeyshines No. 1*, shows one of Edison's assistants dancing. This invention led to the creation of full-length movies by the early 1900s.

Page 21

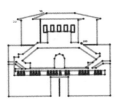

Villa Lewaro

Madam CJ Walker became America's first woman self-made millionaire. She created and sold hair and beauty products for Black women. Her home, Villa Lewaro, was a symbol of hope and inspiration for black women in the 1900's. If she could be successful, then they could too!

Page 23

Order of the British Empire

Alan Turing received this award for his contributions to his country during WWII. It is called the Order of the British Empire. Using his computer, Turing helped crack the Enigma code used by Germany to send secret messages.
This changed the course of the war.

Page 25

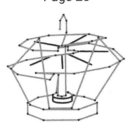

Helicopter

Leonardo DaVinci invented this machine nearly 500 years before the first practical helicopter flew in modern skies. Called the Aerial Screw, four men turned cranks to create enough lift for the machine to rise from the ground.

Page 27

Theory of Special Relativity

This equation demonstrates Einstein's theory of Special Relativity. It means: (E) Energy equals (M) mass times the (c2) speed of light squared. Energy happens when mass moves faster than the speed of light squared.

Page 29

Piano

Mozart's father Leopold taught young Wolfgang Mozart to play the piano when he was 4 years old. Mozart was so successful that he composed his own music by age 5.

Page 31

Reflecting telescope

A reflecting telescope uses light to see objects that are far away. Sir Isaac Newton invented one using prisms. He built the telescope, not to see things in space, but to prove that white light consists of a spectrum of colors.

Page 33

Pilot Goggles

Pilots in the first airplanes sat outside the aircraft. Hats that could be pulled down tightly kept heads warm. Goggles protected the pilot from oil flying out from the engine.

Page 35

Nobel Prize

This is the Nobel Prize. It is awarded for accomplishments in Physics, Chemistry, Medicine, Literature, and Peace. Marie Curie was the first woman to win the prize in 1903. She was the first person to ever win the award a second time in 1911.

Page 37

Beetle

Charles Darwin is best known for his Theory of Evolution. He also loved nature and spent three months in Australia and Tasmania collecting insects. He used his study of insects to support his evolution theory.

Page 39

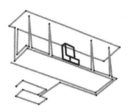

Wright Flyer

Wilbur and Orville Wright invented the first powered airplane. The aircraft, called the Wright Flyer, completed four very short flights at Kitty Hawk, North Carolina in 1903.

Page 41

Flying machine model

Ada Lovelace was a brilliant mathematician. She studied birds to learn more about the mechanics of flight. She designed a steam-powered aeroplane many years before the first steam engine monoplane was attempted.

Page 43

Graphophone

The Graphophone was the first invention that could record and play sound. This machine could record conversations and telephone calls.

Page 45

DNA double helix model

Our cells store DNA in a double helix that curls together. Rosalind Franklin's research proved this model correct soon after it was theorized.

Page 47

Umbrella

In Jane Austen's time, an umbrella protected a woman's skin. Jane Austen believed women should not worry so much about beauty and getting husbands. Women could work and support themselves.

Page 49

Peanuts

Eaten around the world, peanuts are easy to grow. Carver taught farmers to rotate the crops they grow, keeping their fields healthy. He also created over a hundred products using peanuts and made them popular!

Page 51

Music stand

A music stand holds the many pages of music for a performer or orchestra conductor. Mozart conducted the performances of some of his symphonies.

Page 53

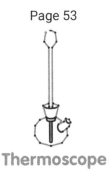

Thermoscope

A thermoscope shows the rise and fall of temperatures. Galileo invented this instrument. This invention led to the creation of the modern thermometer.

Page 55

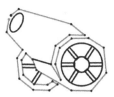

Cannonball

Isaac Newton knew about the laws of motion. To explain how one object can orbit another, he used the example of a cannonball being fired from a cannon on a tall mountain.

Page 57

Wormhole

Wormholes are tunnels in space that allow things to move across great distances very quickly. Einstein theorized their existence, calling them Einstein-Rosen bridges. The theory had a big impact on both science and culture.

Page 59

Brain

Ada Lovelace desired to create a mathematical model of her brain. She wanted to explore and discover how the brain produced thoughts and how nerves created feelings.

Page 61

Chess piece

In 1950, Alan Turing created a computer program or code that could play chess against a human opponent. The program was basic and could "think" ahead two moves in the game. Many consider the program the beginning of A.I.

Page 63

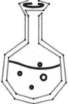

Beaker

When Marie Curie began her work, there were 63 known elements. Curie discovered radium in her lab by separating it from another substance in a glass beaker.

Page 65

Electric lamp

Previous lamps used gas that could explode. Edison's labs created electric lamps that were much safer, making city streets and homes bright across the world.

Page 67

HMS Beagle

A Navy ship, the Beagle took a trip around the world. Charles Darwin was the ship's scientist. He made many observations about evolution on his travels, and when he got home these made him famous.

Page 69

Tesla coil

Tesla coils produce high-voltage, low-current electricity. Tesla built these, and loved creating beautiful currents of energy with them. They were useful components in many of his other inventions.

Page 71

Electric car

Electric cars are cars that run on a battery instead of fuel. Over a century ago, Madam C.J. Walker owned several built by Ford! They're popular now because they're better for the planet than normal cars, so C.J. was ahead of her time.

Page 73

Leaning Tower of Pisa experiment

Galileo dropped balls from the Leaning Tower of Pisa to prove that objects fell at the same speed, no matter how heavy! This changed centuries of scientific thought.

Page 75

HD4 boat

Alexander Graham Bell invented this boat called the HD4.. This water vessel was a hydrofoil. This boat traveled smoothly and quickly on the surface of the water. In 1919 the HD4 set a speed record of 70.86 mph or 114.04 km/h.

Page 77

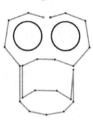

Gas mask filter

Rosalind Franklin's research helped British soldiers during WWII. She made better filters for gas masks based on her studies of coal and graphite.

Page 79

Magnet

As a young child, Albert Einstein was curious about the invisible forces of magnets. Some believe this fascination with magnets sparked his interest in science.

Page 81

Quil

Before the invention of the dip pen, fountain pen, and the ballpoint pen, writers used quill pens (1700-1850). These writing tools are made from the feather of a goose. Jane Austen used these "pens" when writing.

Page 83

Pickax

Darwin was a geologist as well as a biologist. Darwin liked to collect minerals and rocks. He carried equipment, such as a pickax, to collect samples.

Page 85

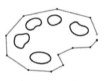

Color Palette

Davinci used a painting palette to mix paint colors. A palette is a flat surface made of wood. When he painted the Mona Lisa, he used brown, blue, and green tones on the palette to create the masterpiece.

"A good attitude is contagious. Pass it on!"

Marie Curie

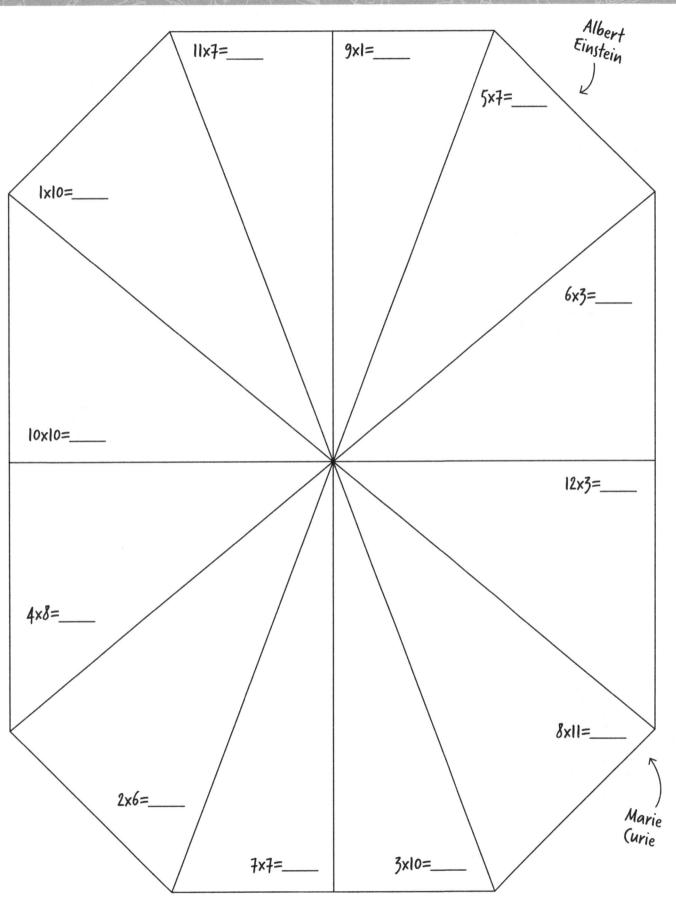

11x7=____

9x1=____

5x7=____

Albert Einstein

1x10=____

6x3=____

Solution on page 113

10x10=____

12x3=____

4x8=____

8x11=____

2x6=____

Marie Curie

7x7=____

3x10=____

"We only get **stronger** when it is **difficult.** "

Madam
C.J. Walker

9x3=_____

1x1=_____

11x4=_____

4x2=_____

2x12=_____

7x3=_____

5x9=_____

3x5=_____

6x6=_____

10x8=_____

Solution on page 113

Thomas
Edison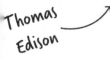

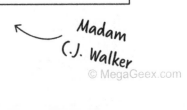 Madam
C.J. Walker

"Don't STOP until you're PROUD."

Rosalind
Franklin

1x10=____	3x5=____	9x7=____	8x4=____	5x7=____	12x5=____	6x9=____

7x8=____

2x11=____

9x10=____

4x7=____

11x4=____

5x5=____

3x9=____

4x6=____

orville Wright

Rosalind Franklin

Wilbur Wright

Solution on page 113

> " It's not about being the best. It's about being better than you were yesterday. "

George
Washington
Carver

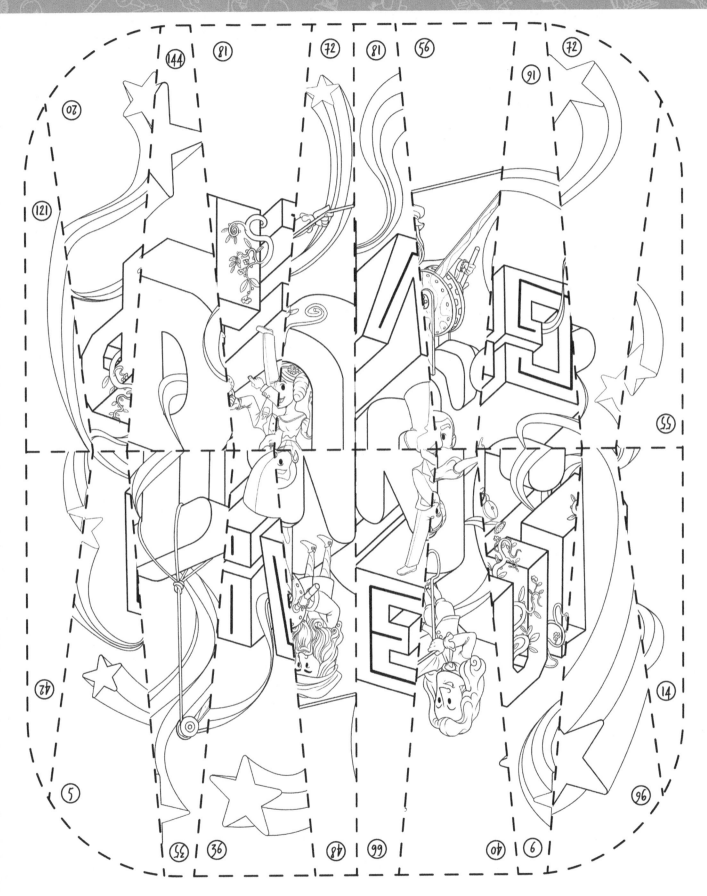

Isaac
Newton

Leonardo
Da Vinci

10x4=____

7x8=____

12x8=____

6x12=____

11x11=
____

12x12=____

8x9=
____

8x6=
____

7x5=____

6x7=
____

5x11=
____

4x4=____

9x2=
____

9x11=
____

3x2=____

2x7=
____

5x1=____

4x9=____

3x6=____

2x10=____

Ada
Lovelace

George
Washington
Carver

Solution on page 113

> # " Just because you haven't found your TALENT yet, doesn't mean you don't HAVE ONE.
>
> **KERMIT THE FROG** "

Wolfgang Amadeus Mozart

Page 99

Page 103

Page 107

Page 111

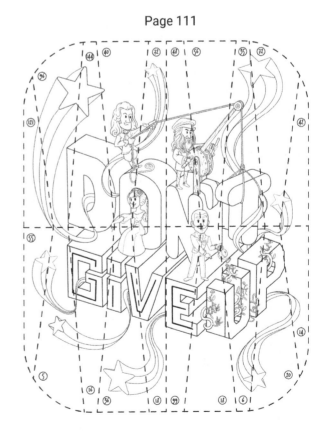

Finished the book?
Well done!

Send us a video and receive a
certificate diploma from Megageex!
support@megageex.com

How can you get more
out of MegaGeex?

Subscribe to our newsletter at
www.MegaGeex.com and follow us on
Instagram and Facebook
to receive free activity pages to inspire
your kids.

🌐 www.MegaGeex.com

📷 MegaGeex

f MegaGeexCom

mega geex

Take learning to a whole new level and bring the Megageex to life with these 3D DIY Books

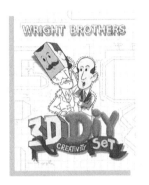  

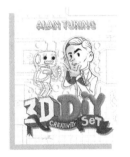   

   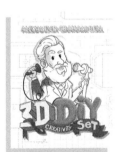

  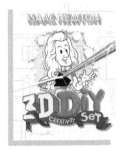 

"Beautiful details. My son loved building it and playing
with all the elements included."

★ ★ ★ ★ ★

Linda N, USA.

Made in the USA
Columbia, SC
15 May 2021